TOTALLY OUTRAGEOUS JOKES

LOVED BY KIDS

Loved by Kids
Tide Mill Way, Woodbridge, Suffolk, IP12 1AP, UK
Copyright © 2018 Imagine That Group Ltd

0 2 4 6 8 9 7 5 3 1
Manufactured in China

Why did the chicken
cross the road?
To get to the other side.

What do baby apes
sleep in?
Apricots.

Why couldn't the
orange get up
the hill?
It ran out of juice.

What is black and
white and read
all over?
A newspaper.

What do
bees chew?
Bumble gum.

Why do bees hum?
They can't remember
the words.

Where do you find
giant snails?
At the end of giant fingers.

Where do sheep get their hair cut?
At the baa-baa shop.

What happened to the cat that swallowed a ball of yarn?
She had mittens.

Why is the sky so high?
So the birds don't bump their heads.

Who was the first underwater spy?
James Pond.

Why do hens watch TV?
To be hentertained.

What do you say if you meet a toad?
Wart's new?

Which animal didn't go in the ark in pairs?
Maggots—they went in apples.

What's green, prickly and goes up and down?
A gooseberry in an elevator.

What goes woof woof tick?
A watch dog.

How do chickens dance?
Chick to chick.

What is a female moth?
A myth.

What do you call a sleeping bull?
A bulldozer.

How do you keep an elephant from smelling?
Tie a knot in its trunk.

What do you call a high rise home for pigs?
A styscraper.

Where do pigs sleep?
In hammocks.

4

What do birds
watch on TV?
The feather
forecast.

What's the most
famous fish?
The starfish.

What do you give
a pig with a
sore throat?
Oinkment.

"Knock! Knock!"
"Who's there?"
"Lettuce."
"Lettuce who?"
"Lettuce in and you'll
find out."

What can you serve but not eat?
A tennis ball.

Where do you
pick up bees?
At a buzz stop.

How does Jack
Frost get to work?
By icicle.

What do you call a spider with no legs?
A currant.

What is the same size as an elephant but weighs nothing?
An elephant's shadow.

What do you get if you cross a clock with a joker?
A laugh a minute.

Why do cows have bells?
Because their horns don't work.

What is the best advice to give a worm?
Sleep late.

What do you get if you cross a mouse with a bar of soap?
Bubble and squeak.

What did the traffic light say to the car?
Don't look now, I'm changing.

Why aren't barbers ever late for work?
Because they know all the short cuts.

What do you get if you sit under a cow?
A pat on the head.

What's the laziest mountain in the world?
Mount Ever-rest.

What nuts can you hang pictures on?
Walnuts.

What has an eye but can't see?
A needle.

How do you join the police force?
Handcuff them together.

What sort of bow is impossible to tie?
A rainbow.

What did the lollipop say to the boy?
"Hello, sucker."

7

What did the envelope say to the stamp?
Stick with me and we'll go places.

Did you hear the joke about the trash can?
It's a load of rubbish.

Did you hear about the man who washed his front doorstep?
He broke his washing machine.

What has four legs and a trunk?
A mouse on vacation.

When is an English teacher like a judge?
When she hands out long sentences.

What's the best thing to put in a pizza?
Your teeth.

What is
a mermaid?
A deep-shelfish.

How do you get
a ghost to lie
perfectly flat?
You use a spirit level.

Why did the pilot land the airplane
on the house roof?
Because the man had left the landing
light on.

What did the mother ghost say to the naughty
baby ghosts?
Speak when you're spooken to.

Did you hear about the
cross-eyed teacher?
He had no control over
his pupils.

Why wouldn't the
skeleton go to school?
Because his heart wasn't
in it.

9

Did you hear about the brilliant geography teacher?
He had abroad knowledge of his subject.

What do you get if you cross a helicopter with a shark?
A helichomper.

What kind of ghosts haunt hospitals?
Surgical spirits.

What does a cow with hiccups give you?
A milk shake.

Why did the math teacher marry the school cleaner?
Because she swept him right off his feet.

What did the big telephone say to the little telephone?
You're too young to be engaged.

Did you hear about the two peanuts walking through Times Square?
One was a-salted.

What do you get if
you cross a mouse
with an
apple core?
A pip squeak.

Why did the teacher
have her hair in
a bun?
Because she had her
nose in a hamburger.

What position do
ghosts play in soccer?
Ghoulie.

Why did the robot
act stupid?
Because he had a
screw loose.

What goes red, green, red,
green, red, green?
A frog in a liquidizer.

What goes 99 bonk,
99 bonk?
A centipede with a
wooden leg.

What's small,
green and does
good deeds?
A cub sprout.

11

How does a monster count to 13?
By using its fingers.

What's worse than finding a maggot in an apple?
Finding half a maggot.

What time is it when an elephant sits on your fence?
Time to get a new one.

Why do stupid people eat biscuits?
Because they're crackers.

Who delivers gifts to baby sharks at Christmas?
Santa Jaws.

What did the sea say to the sand?
Nothing, it just waved.

What unlocks a house at Christmas?
A turkey.

Where do fish keep their money?
In the river bank.

12

What is the definition
of a doughnut?
A crazy millionaire.

Why did the tortoise
cross the road?
To go to the shell shop.

What did the man say
when he walked into
the bar?
Ouch!

What do vampires
like for lunch?
Fangfurters.

What's the smallest ant in the world?
An infant.

What's the heaviest
part of a fish?
Its scales.

Jane: "Knock, knock."
Sue: "Who's there?"
Jane: "See, you've
forgotten me already."

What's the best place
to find diamonds?
In a pack of cards.

Which side of a cup
is the handle on?
The outside.

13

Why was the little bird expelled from school?
She kept playing practical yolks.

What do you do with a blue banana?
Try and cheer it up.

Why did the bus stop?
Because it saw a zebra crossing.

My sister is so dim she thinks that a cartoon is a song you sing in a car.

What is white, furry and has a hole in the middle of it?
A polo bear.

Why did the tomato blush?
Because it saw the salad dressing.

Tom: "It's raining cats and dogs."
Jim: "Well, make sure you don't step in a poodle."

What goes zzub, zzub?
A bee flying backwards.

Why do vampires never get fat?
They eat necks to nothing.

Why were the two flies playing soccer in the saucer?
They were practicing for the cup.

Did you hear the joke about the butter?
I better not tell you, you might spread it.

Did you hear about the hyena who swallowed a gravy cube?
He made a laughing stock of himself.

Why did the teacher put on her sunglasses?
Because her pupils were too bright.

What's big, grey and fast?
An elephant on roller skates.

What house weighs the least?
A lighthouse.

What does a headless horse rider ride?
A nightmare.

Did you hear the
joke about the
high wall?
I'd better not tell
you–you might not
get over it.

What do you feed
a dinosaur?
Whatever it wants.

What happens when
a band plays in a
thunderstorm?
The conductor gets
hit by lightning.

Did you hear about
the wooden car?
It had wooden
wheels, wooden
windows and
wooden go.

Why are penguins such
good racing drivers?
Because they are in
a pole position.

Why does a stork stand on one leg?
Because it would fall over if it lifted the other one.

What is a tornado?
Mother nature doing the twist.

What sort of ship does Count Dracula sail on?
A blood vessel.

What do you do with a sick wasp?
Take it to the waspital.

What did the skeleton make in art class?
A skull-pture.

How did the baker get an electric shock?
He stood on a bun and a currant ran up his leg.

Are vampires mad?
Well, they're often bats.

What do cats read every morning?
Mewspapers.

How do you get freckles?
Sunbathe under a sieve.

What fish tastes best with ice cream?
A jellyfish.

17

My dog saw a sign
that said:
Wet Paint—so he did.

Where do cows go
for an evening out?
To the moo-vies.

What do cats like
for breakfast?
Mice Krispies.

What do you call a
woodpecker with no beak?
A head banger.

What's thick, black, floats on water and
shouts "Underpants"?
Crude oil.

On which side
has a chicken got
more feathers?
On the outside.

What runs but has no legs?
A tap.

What's black and white
and makes a lot of noise?
A zebra with a set
of drums.

What is the dead
centre of a town?
A cemetery.

What's red and goes beep, beep?
A strawberry in a traffic jam.

What is a snail?
A slug with a
crash helmet.

What goes through
the water at a 100
miles per hour?
A motor pike.

What wears a coat all
winter and pants
all summer?
A dog.

Why do we plant
bulbs in the garden?
So the worms can see
where they're going.

What happened when
the cows escaped
from their field?
There was udder chaos.

What lives in apples and
is an avid reader?
A bookworm.

What's big, grey and
wobbles at the knees?
A jellyphant.

What do you get if you cross an elephant with a skunk?

A big stinker.

What's round, white and laughs a lot?

A tickled onion.

What do you call a skeleton that's always sleeping?

Lazy bones.

How do you get rid of varnish?

Take away the R.

Why did the monster eat a lightbulb?

Because he needed some light refreshment.

What do you get if you cross an elephant with a mouse?

Big holes in your walls.

What did the stupid monster call his pet tiger?

Spot.

What time did the man go to the dentist?

Tooth-hurtie.

"Doctor, doctor, I think I'm invisible."
"Who said that?"

How does Dracula keep fit?
He plays batminton.

Why did the monster take his nose apart?
To see what made it run.

What do cows have for breakfast?
Moos-li.

What bird is always out of breath?
A puffin.

How do farmers count their cows?
They use cowculators.

What do you get if you cross a cat with a lemon?
A sourpuss.

What's the best thing to give a seasick elephant?
Plenty of room.

21

What do you get if you cross a galaxy with a toad?
Star Warts.

What's the strongest creature in the ocean?
A mussel.

Why was the mother kangaroo cross with her children?
Because they ate chips in bed.

What do you call a man with a seagull on his head?
Cliff.

"Doctor, doctor, everyone keeps ignoring me."
"Next!"

What's a cannibal's favourite game?
Swallow my leader.

What do you call a man with a spade on his head?
Doug.

Why are false teeth
like stars?
They come out
at night.

What's a skeleton's
favourite instrument?
A trombone.

Why couldn't the two
elephants go swimming?
Because they only had one
pair of trunks.

What is a dimple?
A pimple going the
wrong way.

How do you get milk from a cat?
Take away its saucer.

How many skunks does it
take to make a big stink?
A phew!

What two things
can't you have
for breakfast?
Lunch and dinner.

Why did the fly dance on the jam jar lid?
Because it said "Twist to open."

Why are sheep like pubs?
They're full of baas.

What's the best way to cover a cushion?
Sit on it.

What kind of jokes does a chiropodist like?
Corny jokes.

Did you hear about the stupid tap dancer?
He fell in the sink.

What's the best way of stopping a monster from sliding through the eye of a needle?
Tie a knot in its neck.

What is hairy and coughs?
A coconut with a cold.

What do you call a thin mouse?
A narrow squeak.

What does the winner lose in a race?
His breath.

What's the best thing to take into the desert?
A thirst-aid kit.

Why did the crocodile
bite his own tail?
He was trying to make
both ends meet.

What do you call an
angry kangaroo?
Hopping mad.

What do you call a
penguin in the jungle?
Lost.

What do you give
a seasick hippo?
Lots and lots of room.

Where do witches'
frogs sit?
On toadstools.

When is it bad luck to be followed by a
black cat?
When you're a mouse.

How do you stop a
werewolf howling in
the back of your car?
Put him in the front.

What can you make
that can't be seen?
A noise.

What is the
loudest game?
Tennis, because you
need a racket to play.

"Have you any
invisible ink?"
"Certainly, Sir.
What colour?"

What fish can sing?
The tuna fish.

If two shirt collars
had a race, which
one would win?
Neither. It would
end in a tie.

What did the cookie
say as it rolled down
the hill?
"Oh, crumbs!"

What can you keep and give
away at the same time?
A cold.

Why did the skunk
buy a lotto ticket?
He wanted to be
stinking rich.

Why didn't the dinosaur
cross the road?
Because roads hadn't
been invented.

26

What is big, grey and mutters?

A mumbo jumbo.

What happened when the idiot had a brain transplant?

The brain rejected him.

What do you get if you cross a centipede and a parrot?

A walkie-talkie.

What do you call a donkey with only three legs?

A wonky.

What happened to the man who put his false teeth in backwards?

He ate himself.

What game do little ghosts play at parties?

Haunt the thimble.

What's a giant's favourite tale?

A tall story.

A bird in the hand can make a terrible mess.

What did the shy pebble say?
"I wish I was a little boulder."

Why didn't the skeleton jump off the cliff?
Because he had no guts.

What do you do if your nose goes on strike?
Picket.

What do you call a road with diamonds down the middle?
A jewel carriageway.

How many balls of string does it take to reach the Moon?
One if it's long enough.

Where do ghouls go to study?
Ghoullege.

Why are turkeys bad mannered?
Because they always gobble their dinners.

What changes colour every two seconds?
A chameleon with hiccups.

How do you make a
band stand?
Take away their chairs.

Why does a golfer
need a spare pair
of shoes?
In case he gets a
hole in one.

What do you call a man
who's already around
when you want him?
Andy.

What part of a crocodile
weighs the most?
Its scales.

What do you call
an ape that swings
from cake shop to
cake shop?
A meringue-utang.

"Knock! Knock!"
"Who's there?"
"Alec."
"Alec who?"
"Alec a cup of
coffee, please."

What do you call a
zebra with no stripes?
A horse.

What did the puddle say
to the rain?
Why don't you drop
in sometime.

What happens when you throw a green stone in the Red Sea?
It gets wet.

"Knock! Knock!"
"Who's there?"
"Little boy who can't reach the doorbell!"

Why did the plumber go into the garden?
To mend the leeks.

Why are ghosts so bad at lying?
You can see straight through them.

Why is a baby like an old car?
They both have a rattle.

What is a net?
Holes tied together with string.

Why are rivers rich?
Because they have two banks.

What do monkeys sing at Christmas?
"Jungle bells, jungle bells..."

What's small, furry and cuts corn?
A combine hamster.

What's red and
clumsy?
A blood clot.

What smells, has four
wheels and flies?
A garbage truck.

What's a horse's
favourite sport?
Stable tennis.

What is parrot
food called?
Pollyfilla.

What sort of fish can't swim?
A dead one.

Why was the sand wet?
Because the seaweed.

How do fish travel
from one place
to another?
On the whale way.

How long should a
horse's legs be?
Long enough to reach
the ground.

Why are brides
unlucky?
They never marry the
best man.

31

What do you call a
disastrous cat?
A catastrophe.

What do you call five
bottles of lemonade?
A pop group.

Why was the
insect kicked out
of the park?
Because it was a
litterbug.

Why did the
elephant leave the
circus?
He was tired of
working for peanuts.

What do you do if
you split your sides
laughing?
Run until you get a
stitch.

How do fleas travel
from one place to
another?
By itch hiking.

"Doctor, doctor, I've got a little stye."
"Well you'd better buy a little pig."

What do you get if you cross a sheep dog and a bunch of daisies?
Collie-flowers.

Which day of the week do ghosts like best?
Moandays.

What's the difference between a vampire and a cookie?
You can't dip a vampire in your coffee.

Why are four-legged animals bad dancers?
Because they have two left feet.

What do you call a buffalo in a revolving door?
Stuck.

What do you call a deer with no eyes?
No idea.

What do you call a deer with no eyes and no legs?
Still no idea.

Did you hear the one
about the cornflakes?
I'll tell you next week,
it's a cereal.

What would happen
if pigs could fly?
Bacon would go up.

What goes up and
doesn't come down?
Your age.

Which famous artist
used to sit on ice cubes?
Bottichilli.

How do you start
a bear race?
"Ready, Teddy, Go!"

What starts with a T,
ends with a T and is
full of T?
A teapot.

Who invented fire?
A bright spark.

What did Noah use to
light his Ark?
Floodlights.

When does Friday come
before Thursday?
In the dictionary.

34

What's green and
bounces around
the garden?
A spring onion.

"Knock, Knock!"
"Who's there?"
"Boo."
"Boo who?"
"There's no need to
cry, it's only a joke."

How did they know that the shark
victim had dandruff?
He left his head and shoulders on the beach.

Why is gossip like a kiss?
It passes from mouth
to mouth.

What swings from
cake to cake?
Tarzipan.

What's the difference between stork and butter?
Butter can't stand on one leg.

What's big and grey and has
sixteen wheels?
An elephant on roller skates.

What's black and white
and red all over?
A zebra on a sunbed.

35

Why did Robin Hood
only steal from the rich?
Because the poor had
nothing worth stealing.

Why do birds fly
south in winter?
Because it's too far
to walk.

What fruit is
found in a stable?
A strawberry.

What animal do you
look like when you
have a bath?
A little bear.

Why do French
people eat snails?
Because they don't
like fast food.

What do you find in
a gum tree?
A stick insect.

Why do bees have
sticky hair?
They use
honeycombs.

How does a witch tell
the time?
She uses a witchwatch.

If two's company and three's a crowd, what are four and five?

Nine.

Who was the fastest runner in the world?

Adam. He was the first in the human race.

What do you get if you cross an egg white with gunpowder?

Boom-meringue.

What makes a glow-worm glow?

A light meal.

Thieves have stolen a van full of wigs. Police are combing the area.

When did only three vowels exist?

Before you and I were born.

Why did the robber take a bath?

So he could make a clean getaway.

Which bird is always
out of breath?
A puffin.

There were two flies
on the wall, which one
was the bandit?
The one on the border.

Which gorilla
had six wives?
King Henry the Ape.

Why did the lady
throw the clock out
of the window?
She wanted to see
time fly.

Man: "I want a
hair-cut, please."
Barber: "Certainly,
Sir. Which one?"

How do ghosts keep their feet dry?
By wearing boots.

Which two letters are
bad for your teeth?
DK.

What kind of bandage
do people wear after
heart surgery?
Ticker tape.

What do you call a jacket that's on fire?
A blazer.

What do you get if you cross a nun and a chick?
A pecking order.

How do you service
your pogo stick?
Give it a spring clean.

What do you get if you
cross a dog with a
stick insect?
An animal that will
fetch itself.

Why don't mummies
catch cold?
They're always well
wrapped up.

What has knobs on
and wobbles?
Jellyvision.

Why does a witch ride a broomstick at Hallowe'en?
So she can sweep the sky.

"Doctor, doctor, I've got double vision. How can I cure it?"
"Go around with one eye shut."

What do skunks use to keep their fur clean?
Sham-poo.

What's orange and sounds like a parrot?
Carrot.

What happened to the author that died?
He became a ghost writer.

How do chickens communicate?
By using fowl language.

Where should a twenty pound banana go?
On a diet.

"Knock. Knock!"
"Who's there?"
"Ken."
"Ken who?"
"Ken I come in?"

Why do elephants
have trunks?
Because they'd look
pretty stupid
with suitcases.

Why did the crocodile
buy a new scarf?
He wanted to be a
snappy dresser.

Why shouldn't you tell
a secret to pigs?
Because they're squealers.

What do you call a
clock in space?
A lunar tick.

"Waiter, waiter, have
you got frog's legs?"
"No, Sir, I always
walk like this."

When is a blue book
not a blue book?
When it's read.

Which monster eats
faster than all the
other monsters?
The goblin.

What do you call a dinosaur at the North Pole?
Lost.

What do you get if you cross an elephant with a skunk?

A big stinker.

What makes an octopus a good fighter?

He's very well-armed.

What happens if you play tennis with a bad egg?

First it goes ping, then it goes pong.

What's a cheerful flea called?

A Hoptimist.

What do you get if you cross a gorilla, a cow and a python?

A banana milksnake.

What do you get if you cross a pig with a fir tree?

A pork-u-pine.

What do you get if you cross a cookie with an elephant?

Crumbs.

What's always flying and never goes anywhere?

42   A flag.

Why did the nurse creep silently past the cupboard?
She didn't want to wake the sleeping pills.

"Knock! Knock!"
"Who's there?"
"Isabel."
"Isabel who?"
"Isabel necessary on a bicycle?"

"Doctor, doctor, I've got flat feet."
"Get a foot pump then."

What happens if you eat Christmas decorations?
You get tinselitis.

What sort of ball doesn't bounce?
A snowball.

What do you call a dwarf novelist?
A short story writer.

What's the longest night of the year?
A fortnight.

How did the idiot burn his neck?
Ironing his shirt.

How did tap shoes get their name?
They fell in the sink.

Why don't ghosts make good magicians?
You can see right through their tricks.

What was Noah's occupation?
Preserving pears.

Why was the ghost arrested?
He didn't have a haunting licence.

What did one python say to the other python?
"I've got a crush on you."

What do you get if you pour water down a rabbit hole?
Hot cross bunnies.

Teacher: "What's a robin?"
Pupil: "A bird that steals, miss."

Why are school cooks cruel?
Because they batter fish and beat eggs.

How do you spell "mousetrap" using only three letters?
CAT.

"Knock! Knock!"
"Who's there?"
"Atch."
"Atch who?"
"Bless you!"

What should you take if you're run down?
The number of the car that hit you.

What do soccer players and babies have in common?
They both dribble.

Why can't you pull a snake's leg?
Because he hasn't got one.

What do you get if you cross a burglar with a concrete mixer?
A hardened criminal.

Why do lions eat raw meat?
Because they don't know how to cook it.

"Doctor, doctor, I think I'm a clock."
"Well don't get too wound up about it."

What kind of lion
never attacks people?
A dandelion.

Why did the ghost's
pants fall down?
Because he had no visible
means of support.

Why did the pig
cross the road?
Because it was the
chicken's day off.

What's a python's
favourite game?
Snakes and ladders.

"Doctor, doctor, I
think I'm a witch."
"You'd better lie down
for a spell."

What do you call a
wizard from outer space?
A flying sorcerer.

What snakes are
good at sums?
Adders.

What trees do fingers and
thumbs grow on?
Palm trees.

Why did the egg go
into the jungle?
He was an eggsplorer.

Roses are red,
Violets are blue,
I copied your test paper,
And I failed too.

How does a vampire
enter his house?
Through the bat flap.

What did stone age
men like listening to?
Rock music.

What happens to a witch when she loses
her temper?
She flies off the handle.

"Doctor, doctor, I think
I'm a pack of cards."
"Sit down and I'll deal
with you later."

What was the python's
favourite party game?
Swallow my leader.

How do hippos
play squash?
They jump on each other.

What is a gargoyle?
What ghosts take for
a sore throat.

What's the best
way to see a flying
saucer?
Trip up a waiter.

How does a tailor
make his pants last?
He makes the jacket first.

Did you hear about
the VIP bird?
It was given special
tweetment.

What dog smells
of onions?
A hot dog.

What's the
crocodile's
favourite
card game?
Snap.

What did one eye say
to the other eye?
Between you and me
something smells.

What followed
the dinosaur?
Its tail.

Did you hear about the
sick gnome?
He went to the elf centre.

What did the grape do when the
elephant sat on it?
It let out a little wine.

"Knock! Knock!"
"Who's there?"
"Juno."
"Juno who?"
"Do you know what time it is?"

What did the carpet
say to the floor?
I've got you covered.

What tree is always ill?
A sycamore.

What goes through
water and doesn't
get wet?
Sunlight.

What do you call a flea that
lives in an idiot's ear?
A space invader.

49

What capital city
cheats at tests?
Peking.

How can you tell if a
giant is under your bed?
Your nose touches
the ceiling.

Why is history the
sweetest lesson?
Because it's full
of dates.

Why was the Egyptian
girl worried?
Because her Daddy was
a Mummy.

What do you get if you cross a monster
with a cat?
A neighbourhood without dogs.

"Doctor, doctor, I
feel like a pin."
"I see your point."

Why did the skeleton go
to the party?
For a rattling good time.

What can a bottle of soda hold that a million men can't?
A bubble.

Why are skunks always arguing?
Because they like to raise a stink.

Why was the pony coughing?
Because he was a little horse.

What did the spider say to the beetle?
Stop bugging me.

What cake wanted to rule the world?
Attila the Bun.

Did you hear about the bull that went into a china shop?
He had a smashing time.

Why do koalas carry their babies on their backs?
They can't push strollers up trees.

Why did the snake swallow the firefly?
He fancied a light snack.

What makes grass so
dangerous?
The blades.

How does a monkey
make toast?
He puts it under
a gorilla.

What do you get if
you cross a skunk
with a bear?
Winnie the Pooh.

How do you keep a
twit in suspense?
I'll tell you later.

Did you hear about the sheepdog who had
her puppies in the trash can?
It said PLACE LITTER HERE on the front.

Why do bears wear
fur coats?
They'd look silly in
plastic ones.

What training do you
need to be a
trash collector?
None—you pick it up
as you go along.

What did the dog say
to the skeleton?
I've got a bone to pick
with you.

What runs but has no legs?
Water.

What vegetables are
found in boats?
Leeks.

"Doctor, doctor, I feel
like a yo-yo."
"Sit down...sit down...
sit down."

Why was the teenage goat angry
with his parents?
He didn't like being treated like a kid.

Why do cats change their size?
Because they are let out at night and
taken in in the morning.

What do you call a
witch that can't
stop shaking?
A twitch.

Why do kangaroos
hate rainy days?
Because their youngsters
want to play indoors.

What do you call a boy
on a pile of leaves?
Russell.

What is the opposite
of minimum?
Minidad.

What sort of
sweets do pigs
like best?
Swine gums.

What happens if
ducks fly upside
down?
They quack up.

Why do skeletons
drink so much milk?
Because it's good for
their bones.

What's served in
glasses and is difficult
to swallow?
A stiff drink.

Why do so many people like fishing?
It's easy to get hooked.

Why isn't it safe to
sleep on trains?
Because they run
over sleepers.

"Doctor, doctor! I've only
got 59 seconds to live!"
"Wait a minute, please."

Why did the mole give
up digging?
He was tired with the
hole business.

Why is a soccer pitch always wet?
Because the players are always dribbling.

Why did the skeleton run up the tree?
Because the dog was after his bones.

What do mice have that
no other animal has?
Baby mice.

How do you know a
snowman has been
sleeping in your bed?
You wake up wet.

What do you call an ant with a tube of glue?
A stick insect.

How do you cure a headache?
Put your head through a window and the pane will disappear.

Why do witches do well at school?
They're good at spelling.

Why did the man take the duck back to the pet shop?
It had a quack in it.

"Doctor, doctor, I snore so loudly I keep myself awake. What can I do?"
"Sleep in another room."

What did the dentist say when his wife baked a cake?
"I'll do the filling, dear."

What did one bee say to the other bee?
"Swarm in here, isn't it?"

Why did the apple turnover?
Because it saw the jam roll.

"Doctor, doctor, I think I'm shrinking." "Well, you'll have to be a little patient."

What do monsters eat after having their teeth out?
The dentist.

"Doctor, doctor, I think I'm a fly!" "Well buzz off then."

Why did the woman fix her bed to the chandelier?
Because she was a light sleeper.

What has a bottom at the top?
A leg.

Why did the fish blush?
It saw the ocean's bottom.

What do fireflies do first thing in the morning?
Rise and shine.

"Knock! Knock!"
"Who's there?"
"Lettuce."
"Lettuce who?"
"Lettuce in while you read all the jokes."

Why was the musician arrested?

For getting into treble.

What's the heaviest thing in a student's bag?

A pencil–because it's full of lead.

"Mommy, mommy, the other kids keep saying I look like a werewolf."

"Be quiet, dear, and go and comb your face."

What kind of beans do cannibals like best?

Human beans.

What do geese eat?

Gooseberries.

Did you hear about the idiot who made his chickens drink hot water?

He thought they would lay hard-boiled eggs.

Sid: "Who was that at the door?"

Ann: "A man with a wooden leg."

Sid: "Well, tell him to hop it."

What do you call a woman with one leg shorter than the other?
Eileen.

Who never minds being interrupted in the middle of a sentence?
A convict.

"Knock! Knock!"
"Who's there?"
"Dana."
"Dana who?"
"Dana speak with your mouth full."

What relation is a doorstep to a doormat?
A stepfarther.

Why did the chewing gum cross the road?
It was stuck to the chicken's foot.

Why did the strawberries cry?
Because they were in a jam.

"Doctor, doctor, how can I stop myself from sleepwalking?"
"Sprinkle tacks on your bedroom floor."

Did you hear about the soccer team that were so bad the crowd changes were announced to the team?

What lives under the sea and carries people?
An octobus.

What is a ghost's favourite dessert?
Strawberries and scream.

Where do frogs put their coats?
In a croak room.

Where do hamsters come from?
Hamsterdam.

What goes into the water pink and comes out blue?
A swimmer on a cold day.

What do traffic controllers like for tea?
Traffic jam sandwiches.

What has two heads, three hands, two noses and five feet?
A monster with spare parts.

When is a black dog not a black dog?
When it's a greyhound.

Did you hear about the idiot buying some bird seed?
He said he wanted to grow some birds.

What's black and white, black and white, black and white?
A penguin rolling down a hill.

Why are vampires artistic?
They're good at drawing blood.

What has eight feet and sings?
The school quartet.

What kind of monster has the best hearing?
The eeriest.

What did one skeleton say to the other?
If we had any guts we'd get out of here.

What happened when the dog swallowed a roll of film?
Nothing serious developed.

What's a skeleton?
Bones with the person off.

"Doctor, doctor, I keep thinking I'm a pair of curtains."
"Pull yourself together, man."

Why is it difficult to open up a piano?
Because all the keys are inside.

"What's the difference between a letterbox and an elephant's bottom?"
"I don't know."
"Well, I hope your mum never sends you out to post a letter."

Why is it bad to upset a cannibal?
You'll end up in hot water.

What do you get when you cross a dog with a chicken?
Pooched eggs.

What's the rudest food?
Sausages because they
spit at you.

How do you stop a
skunk from smelling?
Hold its nose.

Have you heard the one about the man who
bought a paper shop?
It blew away.

What do ducks watch on TV?
Duckumentaries.

I used to be a werewolf,
but I'm howl right now.

What do golfers use in
China?
China tees.

What do you get
when you cross a
witch with an iceberg?
A cold spell.

What dress does
everyone have but
nobody wears?
An address.

63

Where do zombies go for their jokes?
To crypt writers.

Did you hear about the man who kept his wife under his bed?
He thought she was a little potty.

Why does a witch ride on a broomstick?
Because a vacuum cleaner is too heavy.

What tools do you use in arithmetic?
Mulitpliers.

Why do ghosts like to haunt tall buildings?
Because there's lots of scarecases.

"Knock! Knock!"
"Who's there?"
"Isabel."
"Isabel who?"
"Isabel better than all this knocking?"

What do you call a penguin in the Sahara Desert?
Lost.

How did the firefly feel when its tail fell off?
It was de-lighted.

What room has no walls, no door and no ceiling?
A mushroom.

How do you make a reindeer fly?
Buy it an airline ticket.

What is enormous and has a red face?
A dinosaur with sunburn.

"Knock! knock!"
"Who's there?"
"Egbert."
"Egbert who?"
"Egbert no bacon."

If money doesn't grow on trees how come banks have so many branches?

What do you call a camel with three humps?
Humphrey.

What did the big cobra say to the little cobra?
"You're the spitting image of your father."

Did you hear about the man who sent his photograph to the Lonely Hearts Club? They sent it back and said they weren't that lonely.

What's the best day to fry eggs? Fryday.

When is water musical? When it's piping hot.

How do you save dumplings from drowning? Put them in gravy boats.

How do you knit a suit of armour? Use steel wool.

"Doctor, doctor, I keep thinking I'm a canary." "I can't tweet you. Go and see a vet."

Why do nuns walk on their heels? To save their souls.

What's a lazy rooster called? A cockle-doodle don't.

If you have a referee in soccer and an umpire in baseball, what do you have in bowls?

Goldfish.

What sits at the bottom of the sea and shakes?

A nervous wreck.

"Knock! Knock!"
"Who's there?"
"Genoa."
"Genoa who?"
"Genoa good teacher?"

Teacher: "Jones, you should have been here at nine o'clock."
Jones: "Why, what happened?"

What's grey, buzzes and eats cheese?

A mouse-quito.

What do you call a sick alligator?

An illigator.

What goes right up to a house but never goes in it?

A path.

What Elizabethan explorer
could stop bikes?
Sir Francis Brake.

Man: "This coffee
tastes like mud."
Waitress: "It was only
ground this morning."

What did the
Martian say to the
petrol pump?
Take your finger out
of your ear when I'm
talking to you.

If all the cars in Britain
were pink what would
you have?
A pink car-nation.

Why are leopards no good
at hide-and-seek?
Because they are
always spotted.

Why do you call your
dog camera?
Because he's
always snapping.

What's grey, has twelve
wheels and carries
a trunk?
An elephant, I lied about
the wheels.

What do you do if you find a monster in your bed?
Sleep somewhere else.

What did the man say when he saw a herd of elephants coming over the hill, wearing sunglasses?
Nothing. He didn't recognize them.

Teacher: "Who can tell me where the Andes are?"
Jimmy: "On the end of my armies."

Where did the cat go when it lost its tail?
To the retail store.

Why do gorillas have big nostrils?
Have you seen the size of their fingers?

Did you hear the story about the elephant sandwich?
It's a bit hard to swallow.

Where would you find a prehistoric cow?
In a moo-seum.

What did the two salt cellars say after they'd had a fight?
Shake.

What did the dirt say
to the rain?
If this keeps up my
name will be mud.

What bird lives
down a coal pit?
A mynah bird.

What kind of apes
talk a lot?
Blab-boons.

What do you call
a doctor who's
butterfingered?
A medicine dropper.

Vet: "I'm going to have
to put your
dog down."
Dog Owner: "Why?"
Vet: "He's so heavy
he's breaking my arm!"

What do you call a
nun with a washing
machine on her head?
Sister-matic.

Why did the one-handed man cross the road?
To get to the second-hand shop.

What's the difference between a shark and spaghetti?
A shark won't slip off the end of your fork.

What's the hottest letter in the alphabet?
B, because it makes oil boil.

What type of dog goes into the corner every time the bell rings?
A boxer.

Why did the skeleton go to the party?
For a rattling good time.

Who said "Shiver me timbers!" on the ghost ship?
The skeleton crew.

Why is Dracula so unpopular?
Because he's a pain in the neck.

71

"Knock! Knock!"
"Who's there?"
"Mary."
"Mary who?"
"Mary Christmas."

What girl would you
take fishing with you?
Annette.

What do ghosts have
for breakfast?
Dreaded wheat.

What sits in custard
looking cross?
Apple grumble.

Sam: "My dog's got no nose."
Ben: "How does he smell?"
Sam: "Awful!"

Why did the elephant
eat the candle?
He wanted a light snack.

What is the most
musical part of
a turkey?
The drumstick.

"Knock! Knock!"
"Who's there?"
"Robin."
"Robin who?"
"Robin your house!"

Why do eagles go
to church?
Because they are
birds of prey.

"Doctor, doctor I keep seeing double!"
"Please sit on the couch."
"Which one?"

What does a cat rest his head on?
A caterpillar.

What do you get from a
pampered cow?
Spoiled milk.

What creature is
useful in a car?
A windshield viper.

"Doctor, doctor,
I'm boiling up!"
"Just simmer down."

What do you get if
you cross a vampire
with a mummy?
A flying bandage.

How did a farmer fix
his jeans?
With a cabbage patch.

"Doctor, doctor,
I feel like a
racehorse."
"Take one of these
every four laps."

What do fish take to
stay alive?
Vitamin sea.

Why do elephants
have wrinkles?
Because they don't
like ironing.

How did the telephones
get married?
In a double
ring ceremony.

"Knock! Knock!"
"Who's there?"
"Rufus."
"Rufus who?"
"Rufus leaking and
I'm getting wet!"

Why did the child
study in the airplane?
He wanted a higher
education.

"Knock! Knock!"
"Who's there?"
"Sarah."
"Sarah who?"
"Sarah doctor in the house?"

What language do they speak in Cuba?
Cubic.

What's the most breathless animal in the jungle?
The pant-her.

How do you know when there's an elephant in your bed?
It's got an E on its pyjamas.

Why did the clock get sick?
It was run down.

What do you call a cow eating grass in a paddock?
A lawn mooer.

What do you get if you cross a tiger with a baseball player?
A very nervous umpire.

What happens if you eat yeast and shoe polish? You'll rise and shine in the morning.

What kind of ant is good at maths? An accountant.

Did I tell you the joke about the empty jar? There's nothing in it.

What do centipedes eat for breakfast? Scrambled-legs.

What's black, crazy and sits in a tree? A raven lunatic.

What do you call an elephant on a diving board? A big dipper.

What games do ants play with elephants? Squash.

What flies around your light at night and can bite off your head? A tiger moth.

76

Why was the broom late?
It overswept.

"Doctor, doctor, I keep painting myself gold."
"Don't worry, it's a gilt complex."

What should you call a bald teddy?
Fred bear.

How do you know if your cat's eaten a duckling?
She looks "down in the mouth."

When do mice need umbrellas?
When it's raining cats and dogs.

Why do giraffe's have long necks?
Have you smelt their feet?

What do lady ghosts put on their skin?
Vanishing cream.

What's the difference between a boring teacher and a boring book?
You can shut the book up.

What is the most popular sentence at school?
I don't know.

Where do you send a sick bird?
For tweetment.

What is the smelliest city in America?
Phew York.

What goes oink, clink, oink, clink?
A piggy bank.

What kind of dog wets the floor?
A poodle.

What cheese is made backwards?
Edam.

"Doctor, doctor, I've swallowed a spoon!"
"Just sit there quietly and don't stir."

How do you make a slow horse fast?
Don't feed it.

What looks like half a cat?
The other half.

What do you get if you cross a tiger with a snowman?
Frostbite.

What do vampires gamble with?
Stake money.

What gets bigger the more you take away?
A hole.

Why did the elephant wear sunglasses on the beach?
He didn't want to be recognized.

Why is history like a fruit cake?
Because it's full of dates.

Which bus sailed over the sea?
Columbus.

"Waiter, do you serve crabs?"
"Sit down, Sir. We serve anybody."

If an apple a day keeps the doctor away, what does an onion do?
It keeps everyone away.

"Knock. Knock!"
"Who's there?"
"Abby."
"Abby who?"
"Abby stung me on the nose."

Did you hear the joke about the body snatchers?
I'd better not tell you–you might get carried away.

What do porcupines like to find in their lunch boxes?
Prickled onions.

Why are feet like ancient tales?
Because they are leg-ends.

What's green and slimy and goes dot dot dot dash dash dash?
A Morse toad.

How do you keep cool at a soccer match?
Sit by a fan.

Mother: "Eat up your roast beef it's full of iron."
Danny: "No wonder it's tough."

What's noisy, runs around the field and sleeps all day?
A bulldozer.

Why did the bird cross the road?
Because the worm was on the other side.

What is a kangaroo's favourite time of year?
Leap year.

What happened
when the lion ate the
comedian?
He felt funny.

What happened when
the cat swallowed
a dime?
There was money in
the kitty.

Did you hear about
the monster who ate
bits of metal
every night?
It was his staple diet.

What schoolbooks
help you get fit?
Exercise books.

"Nurse, nurse, I need to see a doctor!"
"Witch doctor?"
"No, a proper one."

What's the difference
between a teacher
and candy?
People like candy.

What's striped and
bouncy?
A tiger on a pogo stick.

Why didn't the skeleton play music in the church?
Because he had no organs.

What do you call a 100 year old ant?
An antique.

How do you hire a teddy bear?
Put him on stilts.

What is smaller than an ant's dinner?
An ant's mouth.

Why did the dog howl?
Because he was barking up the wrong tree.

What do you get when you cross a dive with a handstand?
A broken back.

"Doctor, doctor, I've got a split personality!"
"Well, you'd better both sit down then."

What subject are witches good at in school?
English! Because they're the tops at spelling.

What kind of dog hides
from frying pans?
A sausage dog.

What do you get if
you cross a leopard
with a watchdog?
A terrified mailman.

When do rhinos
have twelve legs?
When there are
three of them.

How do you make a
glow worm happy?
Cut off his tail and
he'll be de-lighted.

What did the dog say to the cat?
Woof, woof! (of course!)

When is water not water?
When it's dripping.

How do sheep keep warm in winter?
By central bleating.

"Knock! knock!"
"Who's there?"
"Francis."
"Francis who?"
"Francis across the
English Channel."

What's bright blue and
weighs four tons?
An elephant holding its breath.

What do you call a Scottish parrot?
A Macaw!

What's full of holes
but can hold water?
A sponge.

Why is a sofa like a
roast turkey?
Because they're both full
of stuffing!

What's the difference
between a tiger and a lion?
A tiger has the mane
part missing.

How do you get a cut-
price parrot?
Plant bird seed!

"Doctor, doctor,
I think I'm a snail!"
"Don't worry we'll soon have
you out of your shell."

What do owls sing
when it is raining?
"Too wet to woo!"

What language do
twins speak
in Holland?
Double Dutch.

"Knock! Knock!"
"Who's there?"
"Arthur."
"Arthur who?"
"Arthur any
cookies?"

What kind of birds
do you usually find
locked up?
Jail-birds!

What do you call a man
floating on a raft in the sea?
Bob.

What happened to
the leopard who
took a bath three
times a day?
He was spotless.

"Doctor, doctor I keep
thinking I'm a nit!"
"Will you get out of my hair?"

86

What is a puppy's
life like?
Ruff.

What is a polygon?
A dead parrot.

"Doctor, doctor I think I'm an adder!"
"Great, can you help me with my
accounts then please?"

When's the best time
to buy a budgie?
When they're
going cheap.

What were Tarzan's
last words?
Who greased this vine?

"Doctor, doctor I feel
like an apple."
"We must get to the
core of this!"

What do you get if
you cross a glow
worm with a python?
A twenty foot
strip light.

Why is life like a shower?
One wrong turn and you're in hot water.

What happened when the Ice Monster fell out with the Zombie?
He gave him the cold shoulder.

If Ireland fell into the sea which part would float?
Cork.

What should you give an orangutan on his birthday?
A big round of ape-plause.

"Doctor, doctor I think I'm a butterfly."
"Will you say what you mean and stop flitting about!"

What do snowmen wear on their heads?
Ice caps.

Who went into the tiger's lair and came out alive?
The tiger.

Where do birds meet for coffee?
In a nest-cafe!

How does a bird with a broken
wing manage to land safely?
With a sparrowchute!

What's black, white
and red all over?
A very angry panda.

"Knock! Knock!"
"Who's there?"
"Snow."
"Snow who?"
"Snow good asking me."

What do you call a
dinosaur with one eye?
Doyouthinkhesaurus.

What do you call a
very rude bird?
A mockingbird!

What do you call a
dinosaur with no eyes?
Iknowheneversawus.

Who invented the first
plane that couldn't fly?
The Wrong brothers.

What do you get if you
cross a Scottish legend
and a bad egg?
The Loch Ness
Pongster.

What did the curtain say to the other curtain?
"Well, I'll be hanged."

What happened when the owl lost
his voice?
He didn't give a hoot!

What do you get if you cross a zombie with
a boy scout?
A creature that scares old ladies across
the road.

What's the best
way to avoid being
troubled by biting
insects?
Don't bite any.

What do you get if you
cross a woodpecker
with a carrier pigeon?
A bird who knocks
before delivering its
message!

What do you give short elves?
Elf-raising flour.

What do baby swans
dance to?
Cygnet-ure-tunes!

Did you hear about
the burglar who fell
in the cement mixer?
Now he's a
hardened criminal.

Did you hear about the
dentist who became a
brain surgeon?
His drill slipped.

Why did the monkey tie banana
skins to his feet?
He wanted a pair of slippers.

What's the easiest way to make a banana split?
Cut it in half.

What did the "just married" spiders call their new home?
Newlywebs.

"Knock! Knock!"
"Who's there?"
"Cook."
"Cook who?"
"That's the first one I've heard this year."

"Waiter, waiter, I'm in a hurry! Will my pancake be long?"
"No, it will be round, Sir!"

How can you tell when it's rabbit pie for dinner?
It has hares in it.

What do you mean by telling everyone that I'm an idiot?
Sorry, I didn't know that it was meant to be a secret.

What happened to Ray when he met the man-eating monster?
He became ex-Ray.

Why was the cannibal excluded from school?
Because he kept buttering up the teachers.

How do you catch
a squirrel?
Climb up a tree and act
like a nut.

"I have two noses, three
eyes and only one ear.
What am I?"
"Very ugly!"

What's as light as a feather
but harder to hold?
Your breath.

How did the Vikings
communicate with
each other?
By Norse code.

"Knock. Knock!"
"Who's there?"
"A lady with a
stroller."
"Tell her to push off!"

Why are pianos
so noble?
Because they are
either upright
or grand.

"Waiter, what do you
suggest for a
quick snack?"
"Runner beans, sir."

What did one flea say to
the other flea?
Shall we walk or take a cat?

Why are
porpoises clever?
They swim around
in schools.

What did the
mouse say when it
lost its front teeth?
Hard cheese.

When do swimming
trunks go ding dong?
When you wring
them out.

What did the carpet
say to the desk?
I can see your
drawers.

What do you call two
witches that share a
broomstick?
Broom-mates.

What's the best butter in the world?
A goat.

How does a ghoul
start a letter?
Tomb it may concern.

What goes hum-choo,
hum choo?
A bee with a cold!

Why did the cat join the Red Cross?
Because she wanted to be a first-aid kit!

"Doctor, doctor my
husband smells
like fish."
"Poor sole!"

Why did the bird cry?
Because it was a
bluebird.

How long do chickens work?
Around the cluck!

Where do Martians
drink beer?
At a mars bar.

"Doctor, doctor I've lost my
memory."
"When did this happen?"
"When did what happen?"

97

"Knock! Knock!"
"Who's there?"
"Hammond."
"Hammond who?"
"Hammond eggs."

What do you get if
you cross King Kong
with a budgie?
A messy cage.

What's black,
yellow and
covered in
blackberries?
A bramble bee!

What's a monkey's
favourite ballet?
The Nutcracker.

Why did the elephant
jump on top of
the house?
Because he wanted
a flat.

What happened to the
man who swallowed
a doorknob?
It turned his stomach.

What do you get when a chicken
lays an egg on top of a barn?
An eggroll!

What kind of
dog chases
anything red?
A bull dog!

What is the definition of a goose?
An animal that grows down as it grows up!

Where do fish go to
borrow money?
To a loan shark!

"Doctor, doctor will this
ointment clear up
my spots?"
"I never make
rash promises!"

What do ghosts dance to?
Soul music!

How do Welsh people
eat cheese?
Caerphilly!

Why doesn't the sea
spill over the earth?
Because it's tied!

What is the most
slippery country in
the world?
Greece!

What is "out of bounds?"
An exhausted kangaroo!

What is hail?
Hard-boiled rain!

Who was the most
powerful cat
in China?
Chairman Miaow!

Why did the cat cross
the road?
It was the chicken's
day off!

"Doctor, doctor what
did the x-ray of my
head show?"
"Absolutely nothing!"

"Doctor, doctor
everyone thinks I'm
a liar."
"I can't believe that!"

"Knock. Knock!"
"Who's there?"
"Phillipa."
"Phillipa who?"
"Phillipa bath,
I'm dirty."

What do you get if you
cross an eagle with
a skunk?
A bird that stinks to
high heaven.

What is a baby bee?
A little humbug!

Why did the reindeer
laze in the sun?
Because he wanted to
tan his hide.

Did you hear about
the idiot karate
champion that joined
the army?
The first time he
saluted he nearly
killed himself.

What is a baby elephant after he is
five weeks old?
Six weeks old!

"Doctor, doctor I'm
having trouble with my
breathing."
"I'll give you something
that will soon put a
stop to that!"

"Knock. Knock!"
"Who's there?"
"Tish."
"Tish who?"
"Bless you."

What do you get if you cross a parrot
with an elephant?
An animal that tells you everything that it
remembers!

Why do the elephants
have short tails?
Because they can't
remember long stories!

"Doctor, doctor I'm
so ugly. What can I
do about it?"
"Hire yourself out for
Halloween parties!"

Why are
fried onions like a
photocopying machine?
They keep
repeating themselves.

Why don't centipedes
play soccer?
Because by the time
they've got their boots
on it's time to go home.

What kind of ghosts
haunt hospitals?
Surgical spirits.

What do you give a
pony with a cold?
Cough Stirrup!

102

What animal always goes to bed with its shoes on?

A horse!

What do you call a pig with no clothes on?

Streaky bacon!

"Doctor, doctor I think I'm a moth."

Get out of the way, you're in my light!

Why was Cinderella thrown out of the school's basketball team?

Because she kept running away from the ball.

"Doctor, doctor I keep seeing an insect spinning around."

"Don't worry, it's just a bug that's going around!"

Why is a fish easy to weigh?

Because it has its own scales!

What do you get if you try to take a ghost's photograph?

Transparencies.

Why is the graveyard
such a noisy place?
Because of all
the coffin.

What do you get if
you cross a ghost with
a bag of chips?
Snacks that go crunch
in the night.

Why are dolphins cleverer than humans?
Within three hours they can train a man to stand
at the side of a pool and feed them fish!

What makes the Tower
of Pisa lean?
It doesn't eat much.

How do you get rid
of varnish?
Take away the R.

"Doctor, doctor I keep
getting pains in the eye
when I drink coffee."
"Have you tried taking
the spoon out?"

Who was the best
actor in the bible?
Samson, he brought
the house down!

Did you hear about the little boy who was named after his father?
They called him Dad.

"Waiter, waiter, I don't like the flies in here."
"Well, come back tomorrow, we'll have new ones by then."

What is an archaeologist?
Someone whose career is in ruins!

What lies on the ground 100 feet in the air and smells?
A dead centipede.

Did you hear about the mad scientist who put dynamite in his fridge?
They say it blew his cool!

Why did the idiot have his sundial floodlit?
So he could tell the time at night!

Why didn't the banana snore?
Because he was afraid to wake up the rest of the bunch.

"Doctor, doctor I think I'm an elastic band."
"Why don't you stretch yourself out on the sofa there and tell me all about it!"

What do you call a bad lion tamer?
Claude Bottom.

How does the moon cut his hair?
E-clipse it.

Why are fish boots the warmest ones to wear?
Because they have electric 'eels!

Why did the two rhinos crash into each other?
They forgot to sound their horns.

Why is six scared of seven?
Because 7- 8- 9.

What do you get if Batman and Robin get smashed by a steam roller?
Flatman and Ribbon.

When is a car not a car?
When it turns into
a garage.

What do sheep do on
sunny days?
Have a baa-baa cue.

What do they call kittens
in the Wild West?
Posse cats.

Who was the Black Prince?
The son of Old King Cole.

Why did the kangaroo
stop jumping?
Because it was out
of bounds.

What do you call a dog in
jeans and a sweater?
A plain clothes police dog!

What music do fish
listen to?
Sole music.

Did you hear about the
really stupid woodworm?
It was found dead in
a housebrick.

107

Why did the boy put
sugar on his pillow?
So he could have
sweet dreams.

Where do
astronauts keep
their sandwiches?
In a launch box.

"Waiter, waiter, there's
a maggot in my salad!"
"Don't worry, Sir. It
won't live long in
that stuff!"

What do you get if you
cross a worm with a
young goat?
A dirty kid.

What did the skunk
say when the
wind changed?
"It's all coming back
to me now."

What sort of animal
is a slug?
A snail with a
housing problem.

Man: (tucking into
sandwich): "This
bread is nice and
warm."
Wife: "So it should be,
the cat's been sitting
on it all day."

What has one horn and
gives fresh milk?
A milk truck.

Why was the
centipede late?
Because she was
playing this little piggy
with her baby.

"Doctor, doctor, I think
I'm a billiard ball."
"Sorry, you'll have to go
to the end of the queue."

Did you hear about the plastic surgeon?
He sat in front of the fire and melted.

If cows get milked
what do goats get?
Butted.

What do you call a
multi-storey pig pen?
A sty-scraper.

Why did the three
wild pigs leave home?
Because their parents
were terrible boars.

"Doctor, doctor, I keep
thinking I'm a mosquito."
"Go away, sucker!"

What did the hypochondriac have written on his tomb?
I TOLD YOU I WAS ILL.

What's the wettest animal?
A reindeer.

How do you catch a vampire fish?
With blood worms.

What do you get if you cross a dog and a skunk?
Rid of the dog!

What do you get if you cross a vampire with a rose?
A flower that goes for your throat when you sniff it.

Roses are red,
Violets are pink,
There's an octopus in the bath,
So I'll have to wash in the sink!

"Doctor, doctor, three beer kegs have just fallen on me."
"Don't worry, it was light ale."

110

"Doctor, doctor, I've broken my arm in two places."
"Well, don't go back there again."

Did you hear about the tailor who made his pants from sun-blind material?
Every time the sun came out, his pants rolled down.

Why is a Christmas tree like a bad knitter?
They both drop their needles.

What do you call a flying policeman?
A helicopper.

What animal drives a motor car?
A road hog.

What is red, sweet and bites people in the neck?
A Jampire!

111

What's big and grey and never gets to dance?
Cinderelephant.

What does an accountant at the police station do?
Count the coppers.

What did the zombie get a medal for?
Deadication.

Where do baby fish go?
To plaice-school.

What do you get if you cross a skeleton with peanut butter?
Extra crunchy peanut butter.

Why do seagulls live by the sea?
Because if they lived by the bay they'd be bagels.

Which is the best hand to write with?
Neither, it's best to write with a pen.

112

How can you stop a
cold going to
your chest?
Tie a knot in your neck.

What was King Arthur's
court famous for?
Its knight life.

What can lizards do
that snakes can't do?
Stretch their legs.

Teacher: "Which
family does the
octopus belong to?"
Pupil: "No one in our
street, miss."

What would happen if tarantulas
were as big as horses?
If one bit you you could ride it to hospital.

What do you call a
musical spider?
A guitar-arantula.

Who was the skeleton
in the cupboard?
The winner of last
year's hide and seek.

"Knock! Knock!"
"Who's there?"
"Snow."
"Snow who?"
"Snow good asking me."

What did one goat say to the other goat? "I wish you'd stop butting in."

Doctor: "You've got a nasty chill, you must avoid draughts for a week or two."
Patient: "Can I play ludo instead?"

Which side of a tiger has the most fur? The outside.

What stars go to jail? Shooting stars.

How do you join Dracula's club? Send in your name, address and blood group.

What do you get if you cross a bee with a skunk? Something that stings and smells.

Where does a sick
ship go?
To the dock.

What rooms don't
skeletons like?
Living rooms.

Did you hear about the man who stole
a lorry load of prunes?
He's been on the run for a week.

Why did the hazelnut
go out with a prune?
Because he couldn't
find a date.

Why did the doll
blush?
Because she saw the
teddy bear.

"Doctor, doctor, I
think I'm a banana."
"Well slip over there
and peel off
your clothes."

"Knock! Knock!"
"Who's there?"
"Corah."
"Corah who?"
"Corah wish I had a
front door like this!"

115

"Doctor, doctor, I feel like a sheep."
"That's baaaa-d!"

"Knock! Knock!"
"Who's there?"
"Al."
"Al who?"
"Al give you a kiss if you open the door!"

Patient: "Well, Doctor, how do I stand?"
Doctor: "I don't know, it's a miracle."

What's green, has four legs and two trunks?
Two seasick tourists.

What goes at 300 mph on a washing line?
Honda pants.

When is an operation funny?
When it leaves the patient in stitches.

Why did the man put a net over his head?
Because he wanted to catch his breath.

116

Ten cats were in a boat and one jumped out. How many were left?
None, they were all copycats.

What is a female monster's favourite saying?
Demons are a girl's best friend.

How many witches can you fit in an empty coffin?
One. After that it isn't empty any more.

Little sausage dog,
Crossing the street,
Here comes a motor car,
Now it's sausage meat.

What do you get when you cross an ocean with a comedian?
Waves of laughter.

What is a myth?
A female moth.

Teacher: "Why do you always fail your tests?"
Pupil: "Because I keep getting the wrong exam paper."

What did the policeman say when he saw three angels?
"Halo, halo, halo!"

Why do mosquitoes hum?
Because they have forgotten the words.

Which fruit is always on a coin?
A date.

What do you do if you find a trumpet growing in your garden?
Root-it-oot.

What kind of shoes are made out of banana skins?
Slippers.

"Doctor, doctor, I feel like an apple."
"It's okay, I won't bite you."

Doctor: You really have acute hearing.
Patient: Thank you, it's real gold, you know.

What's brown
and sneaks around
the kitchen?
Mince spies.

Do robots have brothers?
No, but they have tran-sisters.

What did Batman give
Robin for breakfast?
Worms.

What do you call a
wooden king?
A ruler.

What do you call a dog
with no legs?
You can call it what
you want, it still
won't come.

What bird is
mechanical?
The crane.

Why do nuns walk
on their heels?
To save their soles.

How did the police
find Quasimodo?
They followed a hunch.

Why did the man take a ladder to the party?
Because the drinks were on the house.

What do you get if you cross a frog with a dog?
A croaker spaniel.

What did the stick insect say to his friend?
Stick around.

Why can't you play cards in the jungle?
There are too many cheetahs.

What's the first thing a bat learns at school?
The alphabat.

"Knock! Knock!"
"Who's there?"
"Stan."
"Stan who?"
"Stan back, I'm breaking the door down."

What goes "HA, HA BONK!"
A man laughing his head off.

Who speaks at a ghost's conference?
A spooksman.

120

Which animal is best at giving advice? The skunk—because it always makes a lot of scents.

What do you get if you cross Dracula with Sir Lancelot? A bite in shining armor.

Mother: "What did you learn in school today?"
Suzie: "Not enough, I have to go back tomorrow."

Did you hear the joke about the empty house? There was nothing in it.

What was written on the metal monster's gravestone? Rust in Peace.

Was Dracula ever married? No, he was a bat-chiller.

Bob: "I like your Easter tie?"
Stan: "Why do you call it my Easter tie?"
Bob: "It's got egg on it."

"Doctor, doctor, I think I'm a dog."
"Sit down please."
"Oh no, I'm not allowed on the furniture."

What did the man catch when he went fly-fishing?
A 20-ton bluebottle.

Teacher: "How do you spell wrong?"
Anna: "R-o-n-g."
Teacher: "That's wrong."
Anna: "That's what you asked for, isn't it?"

"Waiter, what's wrong with this fish?"
"Long time, no sea, Sir."

Angry Father: "Who broke the window?"
Tommy: "Ben, did Dad. He ducked when I threw the stone at him."

If twenty dogs run after one dog, what time is it?
Twenty after one.

Why did the lazy man get a job in a bakery?
Because he wanted a good loaf.

122

What do you get when you cross an apple with a Christmas tree?

A pine-apple.

Where does a general keep his armies?

Up his sleevies.

What do you get if you cross a chicken with a cow?

Roost beef.

Why does an ostrich have such a long neck?

Because its head is so far from its body.

What's yellow and sniffs?

A banana with a bad cold.

"Doctor, doctor, I think I need glasses."
"You certainly do, Sir. This is a supermarket."

Why did the man jump up and down?

He'd forgotten to shake his medicine.

What is a mushroom?

The school dining hall.

Why was the elephant's trunk only eleven inches long?
Because if it was twelve inches long it would be a foot.

How do you make a reindeer stew?
Make it wait for hours.

Why did the ant elope?
Nobody gnu.

"Doctor, doctor, I keep thinking I'm a woodworm."
"How boring for you."

Why did the man put corn in his shoes?
Because he had pigeon toes.

What do you call an ant with frog's legs?
An antiphibian.

"Doctor, doctor, I think I'm turning into a frog."
"You're just playing too much croquet."

"Doctor, doctor, I swallowed a bone."
"Are you choking?"
"No, I really did."

Why did the elephant
put his trunk across the path?
To trip up the ants.

What's a French cat's
favourite pudding?
Chocolate mousse.

What ant can you
crayon with?
A crayant.

What did the cat say when he lost all his money?
"I'm paw."

"Doctor, doctor, I dream
there's monsters under my
bed. What can I do?"
"Saw the legs off your bed."

How many ants are
needed to fill an
apartment?
Ten-ants.

"Doctor, doctor, I
keep thinking I'm an
electric eel."
"How shocking."

Why is it funny to see a
boy run a mile?
Because he really moves
two feet.

Why did the leopards have exactly the same spots?
Because one of them was a copy-cat.

Did you hear about the burglars who stole a calendar?
They got six months each.

Father: "What position do you play in the school football team?"
Son: "The coach said I'm the main drawback."

Why was the crab arrested?
It kept pinching things.

Why don't midfielders like going on planes?
Because they might be put on the wings.

"Knock! Knock!"
"Who's there?"
"Sam."
"Sam who?"
"Sam Francisco, here I come!"

What did one wall say to the other wall?

"I'll meet you at the corner."

"Knock! Knock!"
"Who's there?"
"Anna."
"Anna who?"
"Annanother thing, how long do I have to keep knocking!"

Did you hear about the girl who dreamed she was eating a giant marshmallow?
When she woke up in the morning her pillow was gone.

What wears shoes but has no feet?
A sidewalk.

What's got two legs, two arms and is good on a dark night?
A light-headed man.

"Knock! knock!"
"Who's there?"
"Felix."
"Felix who?"
"Felix my lolly I'll punch him on the nose."

What do you get if you cross a rocket with a kangaroo?
A space shuttle that makes short hops.

127

Have you ever seen a duchess?

Yes, it's the same as an English "s!"

"Is this a second hand shop?"

"Yes, Sir."

"Good. Can you fit one on my watch please."

Did you hear about the mad scientist who invented a gas that could burn through anything?

Now he's trying to invent something to hold it in.

"Knock! Knock!"

"Who's there?"

"Ammonia."

"Ammonia who?"

"Ammonia little girl and I can't reach the door."

Why did the angel lose her job?

She had harp failure.

Why does it snow in winter?

Because the snow would melt in summer.

128

What is the most expensive dog?
A deerhound.

What is the warmest tree?
A fir tree.

What happens if you cross a turkey with an octopus?
Everyone gets a leg at Thanksgiving.

How do you stop a dog from digging holes in your garden?
Hide his spade.

Why do mice need regular oiling?
To stop them from squeaking.

What do elephants say when their calves misbehave?
"Tusk, tusk!"

Where do all good turkeys go when they die?
To oven.

Why is the letter "r" like Christmas?
It comes at the end of December.

What do a dog and a tree have in common?
Bark.

129

"Waiter, waiter, you've got your thumb on my steak!" "I know, Sir, I don't want it to fall on the floor again."

What does a deaf fisherman need? A herring aid.

"Knock! Knock!"
"Who's there?"
"Irish stew."
"Irish stew who?"
"Irish stew in the name of the law."

"Waiter, this chicken has dots on it." "It's okay, Sir, it's only chicken pox."

When is a boat like a heap of snow? When it comes a-drift.

What do you call someone who makes half size models of fish? A scale modeller.

What do you call a chocolate that teases small animals? A mole-teaser.

What's worse than an eagle that's afraid of heights? An elephant with a blocked nose.

What do you call a very fast horse?

A gee gee whizz.

What do you call a musical instrument that is played by two teams of twenty people?

A piano forte.

Why did the soccer pitch end up as a triangle?

Somebody took a corner.

Why was the roadrunner hopping mad?

He ran out of roads.

What do you get if you type www.(and then the whole alphabet) into your computer?

A sore finger.

Dad: "You're sitting for hours in front of that computer. Have you had your eyes checked?"

Son: "No, they've always been green."

What usually happens after a monster lights the candles on his birthday cake?

Someone sends for the fire service.

131

Why did the tennis player have his hands over his ears? He couldn't stand the racket.

Why was the trapeze artist like a pet bird? He was always flying from swing to swing.

Why did nobody like the tell-tale witch? She was a snitch.

What do you get if you cross a skunk and an angel? Something that stinks to high heaven.

What do you get if you cross a psychic with a TV? Tele-vision.

What was wrong with the sick chicken? It had people pox.

Why would the luggage handler make a good detective? He hardly ever loses a case.

Why was the witch at the seashore tasty? She was a sand-witch.

Why are cats' paws so soft? So the mice don't hear them creeping up.

132

Why was the tree too noisy?
Because of its bark.

Girl: "What sort of plant do you have in your hand?"
Other girl: "A palm tree."

What do you call someone who never stops drinking cocoa?
A coco-nut.

Why were the stick insects such great friends?
They were always sticking up for each other at school.

Why was the cat upset?
He was in a cat-flap.

Why is a cat cleaner than a dog?
It washes itself everyday.

What did the fisherman use as a bookmark?
A flat fish—to mark the plaice.

Why was the ghost shy?
He didn't want to make a spectre of himself.

Why were the ghost's teeth horrible?
He was scared to go to the dentist.

Why couldn't the spaceman land on the moon?
It was already full.

What sea creature is good at adding?
An octoplus.

When is the moon heaviest?
When it's full.

How do you make an octopus laugh?
Give it ten-tickles.

What's the difference between lightning and electricity?
Lightning is free of charge.

What do pelicans eat?
Anything that fits the bill.

What time is it when your watch strikes thirteen?
Time to get a new watch.

What does a duck wear when it dresses up?
A duxedo.

134

What do children make that adults can't see?
A lot of noise.

How can you guarantee good weather when you go to the beach?
Go on a Sunday.

How can you tell the difference between a can of tomato soup and a can of chicken soup?
Always read the label.

What happened to the wolf who was put in the washing machine?
He became a wash and werewolf.

What was the Mexican weather report?
Chilli today, hot tamale.

What word if pronounced right is wrong but if pronounced wrong is right?
Wrong.

Why were the lookalike witches confusing?
It was difficult to tell which witch was which.

How do you know if a boat is affectionate?
It hugs the coast.

How do students sail on the sea?
On scholarships.

Why are sheep boring?
They talk constantly – blah, blah, blah.

What did the boy squirrel say to the girl squirrel?
"I'm nuts about you."

What did the Principal do when he saw the school's gas bill?
He exploded.

What's the difference between a sick monster and seven days?
One is a weak one and the other one week!

Did you hear about the woman who lost her budgie?
She called the flying squad!

Did you hear about the ghost that kept making mistakes?
It made "boo-boos!"

Did you hear about the woman who put her bed in a fire? She wanted to sleep like a log!

Did you hear about the mattress robbery? The police "sprang" into action!

Did you hear about the comedian's motorbike? It was a Yama-ha-ha!

Where do astronauts park their spaceships? At parking meteors!

What do you get if you cross a monster and a chicken? Free strange eggs!

Did you hear about the man who crossed a fish and bad breath? He got halibut-osis.

Did you hear about the tree in the math class? It grew square roots.

What do you get if you cross a soccer player with a fish? A goalkipper!

What did the camel say after three weeks in the desert?
"Long time, no sea."

What came after the dinosaurs?
Their tails!

Did you hear about the cat that ate a duck?
It turned into a duck-filled-fatty-puss!

Why didn't the gnome go to work?
He stayed at home for "elf" reasons!

What school subject do snakes like best?
Hiss-tory.

Did you hear about the astronomer who hit his head?
He saw stars!

Did you hear about the broom hand signal?
It was a sweeping gesture!

Did you hear about the man who crossed a dog with a game of soccer?
He played spot-the-ball!

What is yellow and very dangerous?
Shark-infested custard!

Why did the spider buy a computer?
He wanted to make a web page!

Teacher: "What's the Equator?"
Pupil: "It's an imaginary lion running around the Earth!"

What is a cleaner's favourite fairy tale?
Sweeping Beauty!

Why did the mummy cobra have to stay at home with her kids?
She couldn't find a baby-spitter.

What do you get if you cross a sports reporter with a vegetable?
A common tater!

Why are cats bad storytellers?
Because they only have one tale.

Did you hear about the man who crossed a wireless with a hairdresser?
He got radio waves!

What is a skeleton's favourite shellfish?
Mussels!

What did the necklace say to the hat?
"You go on ahead, I'll just hang around!"

What did Charles I say before he was executed?
"Can I go for a walk around the block?"

Which is the longest piece of furniture at school?
The multiplication table!

What did the chocolate say to the lollipop?
"Hello, sucker!"

What did the jack say to the car?
"Want a lift?"

What is a composer's favourite party game?
Haydn seek!

What happened after Beethoven died?
He decomposed!

What do you say to a hyena on its birthday?
Many ha-ha-ha-ha-ha-happy returns.

140

What happens when a skunk dies?
It's ex-stinked!

Did you hear about the insect film director?
They call him Steven Spielbug!

Did you hear about the man who crossed a cocoa bean with an elk?
He got chocolate mousse!

What do you get if you cross a lawn with a kangaroo?
A grasshopper!

What's big and grey and always running a temperature?
An illephant.

What was the booby prize at the nudist beach ball competition?
A clothes brush!

Did you hear about the boy who didn't like decimals?
He couldn't see the point!

What do you get if you cross a big dog with an oak tree?
A very loud bark!

141

What do you call a
baby whale?
A little squirt!

Why are surgeon's
so funny?
They have everyone
in stitches!

Did you hear
about the stupid
ventriloquist?
He only performed on
the radio!

What do you sing
to a python on its
birthday?
"For squeeze a jolly
good fellow..."

Why is it good to have
an octopus with you if
you go into battle?
They are well armed!

Did you hear about the
stupid inventor?
He invented colour radio!

What happened
when the man ate his
whiskers?
He got a beard belly!

Did you hear about
the man with a two
foot beard?
He walks on his chin!

142

What is a giraffe's favourite fruit?
Neck-tarine.

What happened when the chicken fell in the cement mixer?
It became a bricklayer!

What happened when the duck lost its voice?
It had to visit the quack!

What happened when the wheel was invented?
It caused a revolution!

Did you hear about the constipated mathematician?
He worked it out with a pencil!

What do you call a pirate who makes lots of mistakes?
Wrong John Silver!

Why did the greedy man want to work in a bank?
He'd been told there was a lot of money in it!

Why did the telephone engineer leave his job?
It was driving him up the pole!

143

What's red and yellow and green and gold, purple and orange and blue?
A chameleon walking across a parachute quilt.

Did you hear about the boy who wanted to be a bus?
Nobody stood in his way!

What did the dentist say to the pie maker?
"Can I do the fillings?"

Why did the mailman get the sack?
To put his letters in!

What do you get if you cross a watch with a hen?
An alarm cluck.

Did you hear about the giraffe that was slow to apologize?
It took him a long time to swallow his pride!

Did you hear about the nervous man who ate caterpillars?
He developed butterflies in his stomach!

Why did the ram run over the cliff?
He didn't see the "ewe" turn!

What do you call
a woman with a
cat on her head?
Kitty!

What do you call a ghost
that haunts a chat show host?
Phantom of the "Oprah!"

Which newspaper do
cows read?
The Daily Moos.

Did you hear about the
miserable dentist?
He always looked down in
the mouth!

Why was the doctor
bad-tempered?
Because he had
no patients!

Did you hear about
the mean oyster?
It was shellfish.

What has a big horn and is
very dangerous?
A motor car!

What do giant snails
use to decorate
their shells?
Snail varnish.

When are hilltops
most crowded?
In "peak" season!

What do you get when you cross a coward with a black bird?
A scarecrow!

How do bees get to school?
By school buzz!

How do teachers dress in January?
Quickly!

"Doctor, doctor, I feel like I'm in some boiled fruit!"
"You are in a jam!"

First man: "I always get new clothes when I'm down in the dumps!"
Second man: "I wondered where!"

Did you hear about the wizard's horse?
It turned into a barn!

What has six eyes and still can't see anything at all?
Three blind mice!

What do you call a man who steals bacon?
A hamburglar!

Why did the fortune-teller pack her job in?
Because she could see no future in it!

Why is a broken machine like a failed doctor?
They don't operate!

What do you call the Moon after a huge feast?
A full Moon!

What do you get when you cross a bee with meat in a bun?
A humburger!

What do you call an Arabian ruler with lots of cows?
A milk sheik!

"Doctor, doctor, I think I'm a television program, a television program!"
"Don't repeat yourself!"

At what time of day was Adam created?
A little before Eve!

What do you get after it has been taken?
Your photo!

Which musicians can
you never trust?
Fiddlers!

What do you call a
man on the floor that
lifts up a car?
Jack!

What do you get
when you cross a
cow with a theme
park ride?
A milk shake!

Where can you
order a dairy herd?
From a cattle-logue!

Did you hear about
the pregnant lady
trampolinist?
She had a bouncing baby!

On which day was the
first Moon landing?
Moon-day!

What does a skeleton
use to ring his friends?
Tele-bone!

What do you call a
blood-sucking bat that
attacks pigs?
A hampire!

What do you use to catch an electric eel?
A lightning rod!

What's yellow and writes essays?
A ballpoint banana!

What do ponies use to send secret messages?
Horse code!

What do you get if you throw your computer in the sea?
Brainwaves!

Which English king introduced wine to the country?
Alfred the Grape!

Why is the letter "K" like the end of a pig's tail?
It comes at the end of PORK!

How do you make a Venetian blind?
Cover his eyes!

How does Quasimodo carry his sandwiches?
In the Lunchpack of Notre-Dame!

What do apes use to toast bread?
A grilla!

What do fish put on their dining tables?
"Plaice" mats!

What do you call a crowd at a ghost soccer match?
Spook-tators!

Did you hear about the two fat runners?
One ran in short bursts and one ran in burst shorts!

What kind of dish holds nothing at all!
A ra-dish!

Why are giraffes inexpensive to feed?
Because their food goes a long way!

Doctor: "When did you first start to think you were a cat?"
Patient: "When I was a kitten!"

"Doctor, doctor, I feel like I'm going bald!"
"You need some fresh air!"

Why is the word SMILES so long?
Because there is a mile in the middle!

Why are teachers and teddy bears similar?
They both watch you with beady little eyes!

What sound do porcupines make when they are kissing?
"Ouch!"

When is a pink school book not a pink school book?
When it is read!

Why are small trees like baby elephants?
They've only got little trunks.

Which vegetable can see the best?
A potato–it has lots of eyes!

What do you call a girl who lives under a cow?
Pat!

What are you going to be when you get out of school?
An old man!

What do you call a young bee?
A bay-bee!

151

What's black and
white and never wants
to grow up?
Peter Panda.

What do you call the
biggest mouse in
the world?
A hippopota-mouse!

How can you tell
a wolf man from
his sister?
His sister has a
shorter beard!

How do we know
owls are smarter than
chickens?
Have you ever heard of
a kentucky fried owl?

"Doctor, doctor, I keep
thinking I'm a guitar!"
"You are highly strung!"

What do you call a cat
that lives in the sea?
An octopuss!

What do you get when
you cross a snowman
and Dracula?
Frostbite!

What do highwaymen
bees call out?
Your honey or your life!

What do you get when you cross an elephant with a kangaroo? Something that causes an earthquake every time it hops.

What do you call a horse in striped pyjamas?
A zebra!

What is the worst cake to have in your tummy?
Stomach-cake!

Why does the sea trust no one?
Because it has often been crossed!

"Doctor, doctor, I feel like a banana!"
"Your skin is peeling!"

What does a poltergeist guard call out?
Who ghosts there?

What travels all around the world yet stays in the same corner?
A postage stamp!

What does a lady monster keep in her handbag?
Hands!

How do vampires like their fish served?
In bat-ter!

What's the difference between a teacher and a train?
The train goes "Chew chew" and the teacher says, "Spit that gum out!"

Who can shave all day and still have a beard?
A barber!

Who has a parrot that squawks, "Pieces of four?"
Short John Silver!

What did it say on the alien's school report?
"This pupil's work is out of this world!"

Why did the teacher yell at Humpty Dumpty?
Because he cracked up in class!

Did you hear about the boy who spent hours on his homework each night?
He kept it under his mattress!

What do foxes put on to keep warm?
Foxgloves!

154

Did you hear about
the school near the
chicken farm?
The pupils picked up
fowl language!

What does a lady
snake do when she
has a cold?
Viper nose!

What do you call a
dance for butterflies?
A mothball!

Why did the farmer
have sore feet?
A tractor ran over
his corn!

When did Adam and
Eve eat the apple?
Before their first date!

Did you hear about the
school trip to Venice?
They came back because
it was flooded!

"Doctor, doctor, my son
has grown another foot!"
"Enter him in to a
three-legged race!"

What do you call bees that
keep dropping things?
Fumble bees!

Why did the spider
test drive a car?
He wanted to take it out
for a spin!

What do skeletons
watch for
entertainment?
Skele-vision!

Why is school like
a shower?
One wrong turn and
you're in hot water!

What did the angry
miller try to do?
Grind his teeth!

Where do gardeners
play snooker!
In potting sheds!

What is a monster's
favourite drink?
Demonade!

Teacher: "Your essay about your dog is the
same as your sister's!"
Pupil: "Yes, it's the same dog!"

Did you hear about the man who never cleaned his glasses? He gave everyone filthy looks!

What do you get when you cross a fish with an elephant? Swimming trunks!

What is a cannibal's favourite day! Chewsday!

What do invisible people say to greet each other? "Nice not to see you!"

"Waiter, waiter, why is there mould on my lettuce?" "You said you wanted a green salad!"

"Doctor, doctor, my hair keeps falling out; give me something to keep it in!" "Here is a box!"

What does the Abominable Snowman call its kids? Chill-dren!

What do you call a one-eyed monster on a bicycle? Cycle-ops!

157

"Doctor, doctor, I want to spend all night under the bed!"
"You are a little potty!"

Why is basketball the most respectable sport?
Everyone looks up to the players!

"Knock, knock!"
"Who's there?"
"Aladdin!"
"Aladdin who?"
"Aladdin the street."

What is brown and makes a noise like a bell?
Dunngggg!

Why did the coach put sawdust on the soccer pitch?
He wanted to stop his team slipping out of the league!

Where do sheep go for a haircut?
The Baaaaaaarber!

How do you stop a rhino from charging?
Take away its credit cards!

Did you hear about the secretary who cut her fingers off?
She wanted to write shorthand!

158

Did you hear about
the turkey that ate
too much?
It was stuffed!

Did you hear about
the virus that went
on vacation?
It went to Germ-any!

Mother: "Did you put out the cat?"
Son: "I didn't even know it was on fire!"

Why did the river
go on a diet?
It wanted to lose a
few ponds!

What is a ghost's
favourite fairground ride?
A roller ghoster!

Where do children learn their ABC's?
At LMN-tary school!

Why did the policeman
work up a tree?
He was in special branch!

What's green and
dangerous?
A frog with a
hand grenade!

What did one teddy
say to the other
after dinner?
"I'm stuffed!"

What's black and white
and red at the bottom?
A badger with nappy rash!

How do you make
a milk shake?
Give it a good scare.

What sleeps at the
bottom of the sea?
A kipper.

How do you speak to a fish?
Drop him a line.

Why was the trout's
piano off key?
Because he couldn't find
the piano tuna!

Why was the pelican
afraid to leave the hotel?
Because it had a big bill.

How do biologists
communicate?
By "cell" phone.

Where do aliens go to
see a film?
To Cine-mars.

Where did Sir
Lancelot study?
In knight school.

What coat do you put on
only when it's wet?
A coat of paint.

How do you make a Swiss roll?
Lie him on his side and push him down the hill.

What is a falsehood?
A fake hat.

Why are
Martians green?
Because they forgot
to take their
travel-sickness tablets.

How do young
spooks prefer
their eggs?
Terrifried.

What do you call
an area where
ghosts live?

Why were the witches on strike?
They wanted sweeping reforms.
A terrortory.

What do ghosts wear if they're short-sighted?
Spooktacles.

What do you call a bumble bee with a quiet buzz?
A mumble bee.

What sort of ball doesn't bounce?
A snowball.

What do you call a flying skunk?
A smellacopter.

Which animal is always banned from competitions?
The cheetah.

What is the correct name for a water otter?
A kettle.

"Doctor, doctor, I keep thinking I'm a caterpillar."
"Don't worry you'll soon change."

"Who was that at the door?"
"A man with a drum."
"Tell him to beat it!"